Animals
of Africa

by Lisa Norby

Table of Contents

Introduction

Imagine sitting in a boat and floating down a peaceful river. Suddenly, a large animal comes out of the water a few feet away. It's a hippopotamus (hih-puh-PAH-tuh-mus)!

The Age of Dinosaurs		The Age of Mammals		
206 million years ago to 65 million years ago		65 million years ago to the present		
	206 million years ago	65 million years ago		40 million years ago
	Dinosaurs flourished and birds first appeared. Then, 65 million years ago, dinosaurs became extinct.	Early elephants, rhinos, monkeys, and apes		Earliest ancestors of the great cats; some mammals grew very large

Visitors to Africa's wildlife parks often feel as if they are stepping back in time. They see the land much as it was hundreds of years ago.

That may seem like a long time to us, but scientists think in terms of thousands of years, even millions of years.

Over millions of years, Earth's climate has also gone through many changes. The changes continue today.

Animal life changes along with the climate. Some animals die out. When the last animal of its kind dies, that animal is said to be **extinct** (ik-STINGKT).

In this book, you will read about some of the animals that live in Africa today. You will also learn about some that lived long, long ago, but are now extinct.

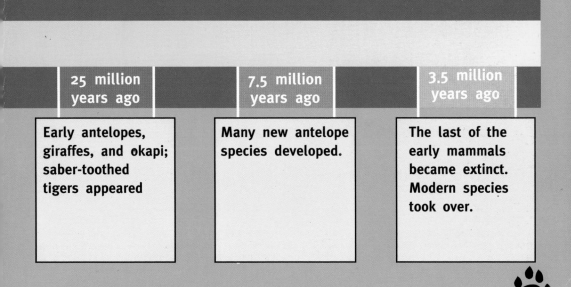

25 million years ago	7.5 million years ago	3.5 million years ago
Early antelopes, giraffes, and okapi; saber-toothed tigers appeared	Many new antelope species developed.	The last of the early mammals became extinct. Modern species took over.

Ancient Fish and Fossils

In 1938, a South African fishing boat caught a strange-looking fish. An official from a nearby museum was called in to take a look. She was amazed. The fish was a coelacanth (SEE-luh-kanth). Everyone thought it had been extinct for eighty million years!

▼ Coelacanths still live in the oceans today. This one was caught in 2001.

Fossils

Most animals that lived millions of years ago are long gone. What we know about them comes from fossils (FAH-sulz).

Once in a while, the body of a dead animal gets pressed into wet sand or mud. Over a very long period of time, the sand or mud turns to stone. Sometimes the bones do, too.

▲ If fossil hunters are very lucky, they may find a whole skeleton.

Usually all fossil hunters find is the imprint of an animal. ▶

Elephants make good fossils because they have strong, heavy bones. This is a computer model made by using a fossilized skeleton found in Africa a few years ago. It looks like a modern rhinoceros (ry-NAH-suh-rus), but it is actually related to the elephant.

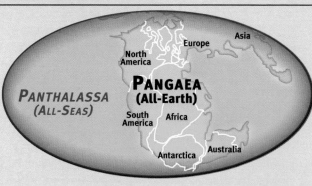

About two hundred and fifty million years ago, most of the land on Earth was united in one big **continent** (KAHN-tih-nent), called Pangaea (pan-JEE-uh).

▲ land on Earth before it broke into pieces

Over a very long period of time, Pangaea broke into pieces. The pieces drifted apart to create the seven continents of Earth today.

The climate was warm and wet. Much of Africa was soft, wet, and swampy.

CAREERS IN SCIENCE

A scientist who studies fossils is a paleontologist (pay-lee-ahn-TAH-luh-jist). Teams of paleontologists spend months digging for fossils. Usually, all they find are a few bones and bits of rock. Back home in their labs, they will try to figure out what the living animal looked like.

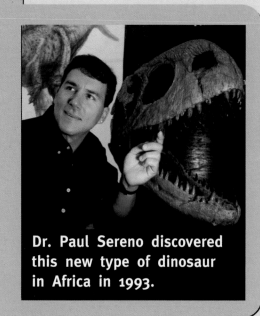

Dr. Paul Sereno discovered this new type of dinosaur in Africa in 1993.

▲ At first, mammals were small. This early member of the elephant family was about the size of a pig.

Mammals

The dinosaurs became extinct about sixty-five million years ago. No one is really sure why. Mammals (MA-mulz) took their place as the largest animals on Earth. What makes an animal a mammal?

Female mammals produce milk to feed their young. A few mammals lay eggs, but most give birth to live young.

Mammals are warm-blooded animals whose bodies are covered with hair. To keep their body temperatures high, they need to eat a lot.

▼ Brachiosaurus (bra-kee-uh-SOR-us) lived in Africa and North America. From the tip of its tail to its nose it was about seventy-five feet long!

7

The earliest mammals were tiny and ate insects. Once the dinosaurs were gone, many new **species** (SPEE-sheez) of mammals appeared. Here are what some of them looked like.

▲ Homotherium (hoh-moh-THEER-ee-um) was an early cat with dangerous curved teeth.

Megazostrodon ▶ (meh-guh-ZOH-struh-dahn) lived in Africa about 200 million years ago.

Agriotherium (ag-ree-oh-THEER-ee-um) was a very large bear. There are no bears left in Africa today. ◀

▲ Percrocuta (per-KROH-koo-tuh) was a larger, early relative of the hyena (hy-EE-nuh).

Forty million years ago, the climate started to cool. Many new kinds of mammals appeared. Some of them were very large and fierce looking. A deep trench called the Great Rift Valley opened up in East Africa.

▲ This giant warthog has a name that's a real mouthful. It's called Metridiochoerus (meh-trih-dee-AH-ker-us).

1 SOLVE THIS

Victoria Falls is 355 feet (108 meters) above the Zambezi (zam-BEE-zee) River. It is part of the Great Rift Valley. If you were standing on the top floor of Chicago's Willis Tower, you would be 1,430 feet (almost 436 meters) above the street. About how many times the height of Victoria Falls is the Willis Tower?

Why did so many new kinds of mammals appear? One reason may have been the climate. Earth was cooler than it had been in the time of the dinosaurs.

Mammals are warm-blooded. They could survive more easily in cooler weather. They could stay active. They could look for the food they needed to keep warm.

Some early African mammals were large, fierce-looking hunters.

Some mammals were plant-eaters. They had many ways to get enough food for themselves.

One group of early mammals had a stretched out nose, or trunk. They were cousins of today's elephant. The earliest animal of this group was the size of a pig. Later on, the animals with trunks became very big.

Many of the early mammals became extinct two or three million years ago.

▼ Dinofelis (dy-noh-FEE-lis) was a meat eater. Its name means "giant cat."

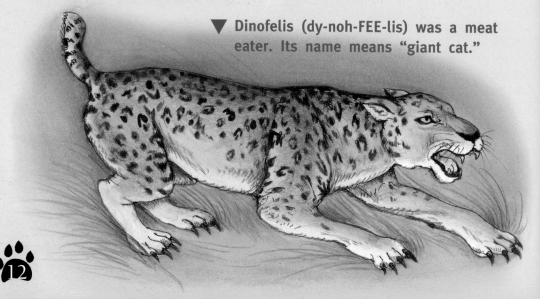

▲ Platybelodon (pla-tee-BEH-loh-dahn) used its flat trunk to shovel weeds off lake bottoms.

▼ Moeritherium (mee-rih-THEER-ee-um) was an early member of the elephant group. It lived in and around swamps.

Where and How Animals Live

Mammals are all alike in some ways. But they are very different from each other, too. Their size, shape, and other features allow them to adjust to their surroundings, or **environment** (in-VY-run-ment). The special ways that animals adjust to their surroundings are known as **adaptations** (a-dap-TAY-shunz). Let's take a look at some animals and learn how they have adapted.

▼ The spotted hyena is a good example of adaptation. It has powerful jaws and can run fast for miles to catch prey. It will eat almost anything to survive, including dead animals—bones and all.

IT'S A FACT

The spotted hyena is also known as "the laughing hyena." Its call sounds like strange laughing.

The giraffe's most important adaptation is its long neck. At eighteen feet tall, the giraffe can reach the tender leaves at the tops of trees. It has an extra-large heart that pumps blood up to its brain.

▲ The naked mole rat is adapted to life underground. It uses its big front teeth for digging tunnels and eating roots.

▼ wildebeest

The wildebeest (WIL-deh-beest) is just one of seventy-three kinds of African antelope. All of them eat grass. But they are adapted in different ways.

Smaller antelopes, such as the suni (SOO-nee), live around trees or thick bushes. This helps keep them safe from predators.

Larger antelopes often have some way to signal to the herd that a lion is near. The impala (im-PA-luh) has black and white stripes near its tail.

The stripes are easy to see when the impala runs. When the klipspringer (KLIP-sprin-ger) leaps into the air, white hairs on its back stand straight up. When other animals see those signals, they run away, too.

The impala is adapted ▲ to its environment.

◄ The leopard is an excellent hunter.

Desert
Grassland
Rain forest

SAHARA

AFRICA

ATLANTIC OCEAN

INDIAN OCEAN

N
W   E
S

0   1,000 MILES

0   1,000 KILOMETERS

The Hunters and the Hunted

The leopard is the greatest hunting cat. It stores its food in the branches of trees, where other animals can't steal it. The leopard can also live in different **habitats** (HA-bih-tats). It can be found everywhere in Africa, except deep in the Sahara Desert.

▲ Africa has three main regions: To the north is the Sahara (suh-HAR-uh), the world's largest desert. Central and southern Africa are divided between forests and grasslands. Those two regions are where most African animals live.

17

Herds of peaceful, plant-eating animals live on the grasslands. But predatory animals are lurking. They wait for a chance to attack a grass eater who is slow or careless.

Lions live and hunt in groups called prides. Mostly they eat antelopes and zebras. But they can bring down larger prey. Even a giraffe is not too big for lions!

▲ The lion is well **camouflaged** (KA-muh-flahjd). Its fur is the same yellowish color as dry grass, so it is hard to see. It is easy for a lion to sneak up on its prey.

Hooves and Horns

Some antelopes use their horns to protect themselves. The giant sable can spear a lion with its long, curved horns.

Even antelope hooves are adapted to different living conditions. One species that lives near water has flat hooves that are good for walking in mud. Another has small, neat hooves which are perfect for jumping from rock to rock.

◀ giant sable

▲ Antelopes have perfect hooves for each habitat.

One Big Bird

The ostrich is adapted to life on the grasslands. At 250 pounds, it is too heavy to fly. But the ostrich can run very fast. If a lion goes after an ostrich, it will probably be sorry. The ostrich can kick hard with its long, muscular legs.

Ostriches often mix with herds of antelope and zebras. The ostrich can see very well. But antelopes and zebras have a better sense of smell. They warn one another of danger.

2 SOLVE THIS

An ostrich can run at a steady speed of about 30 miles (about 48 kilometers) per hour. How far can it run in one minute? In five minutes?

▲ African ostrich

The Forests

The rain forests of Africa are full of strange and unfamiliar animals. It is easy to hide in the thick greenery.

IT'S A FACT

There are no such animals as black panthers. They are just leopards with black fur. About one out of every twenty leopards is born with black fur.

▲ Up until 100 years ago, scientists weren't sure the okapi (oh-KAH-pee) really existed. It is a relative of the giraffe.

▲ black leopard

The slow-moving mother potto ▶ (PAH-toh) and her baby cling to a tree branch. They spend their lives in the trees.

Chimpanzees (chim-pan-ZEEZ) are probably the best-known forest animals. They are very smart and even use simple tools. They can stick a twig inside a termite (TER-mite) mound. When they pull it out, it is covered with tasty insects!

▲ chimpanzees

Sometimes chimps hunt monkeys for food. One troop of chimps even waged a "war" against another troop of chimps. But for the most part, they are peaceful and playful.

▲ Jane Goodall

They Made a Difference
Jane Goodall

Jane Goodall's childhood dream was to see Africa. When she became an adult, her dream came true. She studied chimps in the wild for many years. Goodall became the world's number one expert on how wild chimpanzees act. We know much about these amazing animals because of her work.

Gorillas live at the forest's edge. For the most part, they are peaceful, easy-going animals. Gorillas build sleeping nests out of leaves and branches. When they are not eating tender plants, they take naps and relax in the sun.

A gorilla family is led by an older male called a silverback. When bothered, a male gorilla will pound his chest and charge. But he usually doesn't attack. He doesn't have to. The gorilla's bluff is enough to frighten off other animals. The gorilla's only real enemy is a human with a gun.

✔ POINT

Reread
Find four adaptations that help animals survive.

gorillas ▲

The Struggle to Survive

A herd of wildebeests has reached the banks of the Maru (MAR-roo) River. Crocodiles wait in the shallow water. Wildebeests usually fear crocodiles. Now, they don't seem afraid. They jump from the high banks into the river.

Crocodiles snap their jaws and strike. Some unlucky animals get pulled under. The rest push on to the other side of the river.

▲ crocodile

Twice a year, up to one million wildebeests **migrate** (MY-grate). They make the hard journey across the Serengeti (sair-en-GEH-tee) Plains of East Africa. At the beginning of the dry season, they leave their grazing lands in the south. In the fall, when the dry season is over, they will return.

When large groups of animals travel this way, they are said to migrate. No one teaches the wildebeests how and when to travel. They follow their **instinct** (IN-stingkt).

Thousands of zebras, gazelles, and other antelopes migrate along with the wildebeest herds.

✔ **POINT**

Make Connections

People are mammals with instincts. What kinds of instincts can you think of?

▲ Every year, tourists travel to Serengeti National Park in Tanzania to see the great migration.

Elephants also have an instinct to migrate. If an elephant herd stays in one place, it can strip the tree trunks bare. The trees start to die. The food runs out.

In the past, the elephants would move on to another area. Today, there are often farms and villages in their path. Many elephants now live inside of wildlife parks.

3 SOLVE THIS

An African elephant can weigh 1,400 pounds (635 kilograms). It eats up to 350 pounds (about 159 kilograms) of food a day.

a. How much food does the elephant eat in one week?

b. If a 100-pound person ate at the same rate according to his body weight, how many pounds of food would he eat in one day?

▲ African elephants in Botswana

Natural environments are always changing. If there is enough rain, animals do well. If there is too little, some will die.

But a wildlife park is not a natural environment. What happens when elephants can't migrate? If they destroy grass and trees, other species will suffer. What should the park rangers do? There are really no good answers.

People have always had a strong effect on the environment. Farmers clear forests to plant grain. Cattle ranches take grazing land away from wild animals.

In many parts of the world, open land for wildlife disappeared long ago. Now Africa is facing the same problem. Many of its animals, including the mountain gorilla, the giant sable, and the black rhino are **endangered** (in-DANE-jerd).

▲ black rhino

Conclusion

Many Africans today have never seen a lion or an elephant. One-third of the people live in big cities. They worry about fighting poverty and disease. There isn't much time left over to think about wild animals.

Still, there is hope for African wildlife. Many countries have set aside land for parks and game reserves. Every year, visitors come from all over the world to see African game. The money they spend helps the animals and people, too.

▼ Most wildlife parks in Africa today are found in the grasslands of the eastern and southern regions.

Answer each question. If you need to, reread the book to find the information.

This early bear species lived in Africa. Are there any wild bears in Africa today?

What modern animal is related to this extinct species?

How does this antelope warn others that danger is near?

This animal has unusual eating habits. Explain.

What makes this animal migrate?

Glossary

adaptation   (a-dap-TAY-shun) a change that helps animals or plants live in a certain place (page 14)

camouflage   (KA-muh-flahj) coloring or patterning that helps an animal blend in with its environment (page 18)

continent   (KAHN-tih-nent) any one of seven large land areas on Earth (page 6)

endangered   (in-DANE-jerd) close to dying out completely (page 28)

environment   (in-VY-run-ment) the air, land, and water where animals live (page 14)

extinct   (ik-STINGKT) no longer existing anywhere on Earth (page 3)

habitat   (HA-bih-tat) the place where a particular animal or plant lives; each habitat has its own kind of climate and land or water conditions (page 17)

instinct   (IN-stingkt) ability to do something without thinking or without having learned it (page 25)

migrate   (MY-grate) to move from one place to another at the same time each year (page 25)

species   (SPEE-sheez) the smallest group of living things that have the same traits (page 8)

SOLVE THIS ANSWERS

1. Page 11
The Willis Tower is about four times as high as Victoria Falls: 1,430/355 = 4 (436/108 = 4).

2. Page 20
.5 mile (.8 kilometer) in one minute, 2.5 miles (4 kilometers) in five minutes.

3. Page 26
a. 2,450 pounds (1,113 kilograms) of food in one week. 350 x 7 = 2,450 (159 x 7 = 1,113)
b. 25 pounds of food (1,400/350 = 4, 100/4 = 25)

Index